Skillet DESSERTS

THE SOUTHERN ART OF SKILLET TO TABLE

Skillet DESSERTS

THE SOUTHERN ART OF SKILLET TO TABLE

hm | books

hm | books

PRESIDENT/CCO Brian Hart Hoffman
VICE PRESIDENT/EDITORIAL Cindy Smith Cooper
CREATIVE DIRECTOR/ART Deanna Rippy Gardner

TASTE OF THE SOUTH EDITORIAL

EDITOR Brooke Michael Bell
CREATIVE DIRECTOR/PHOTOGRAPHY Mac Jamieson
MANAGING EDITOR Josh Miller
ASSISTANT EDITOR Ginny Heard
EDITORIAL ASSISTANT Caroline Russell
COPY EDITOR Avery Hurt
PHOTO STYLIST Mary Beth Stillwell
SENIOR PHOTOGRAPHERS John O'Hagan, Marcy Black Simpson
PHOTOGRAPHERS Jim Bathie, William Dickey, Stephanie Welbourne
EXECUTIVE CHEF Rebecca Treadwell Spradling
TEST KITCHEN PROFESSIONALS Allene Arnold, Melissa L. Brinley,
Kathleen Kanen, Janet Lambert, Vanessa Rocchio, Anna Theoktisto, Loren Wood
TEST KITCHEN ASSISTANT Anita Simpson Spain
SENIOR DIGITAL IMAGING SPECIALIST Delisa McDaniel
DIGITAL IMAGING SPECIALIST Clark Densmore

---

hm
hoffmanmedia

CHAIRMAN OF THE BOARD/CEO Phyllis Hoffman DePiano
PRESIDENT/COO Eric W. Hoffman
PRESIDENT/CCO Brian Hart Hoffman
EXECUTIVE VICE PRESIDENT/CFO Mary P. Cummings
EXECUTIVE VICE PRESIDENT/OPERATIONS & MANUFACTURING Greg Baugh
VICE PRESIDENT/DIGITAL MEDIA Jon Adamson
VICE PRESIDENT/EDITORIAL Cindy Smith Cooper
VICE PRESIDENT/ADMINISTRATION Lynn Lee Terry

Hoffman Media
1900 International Park Drive, Suite 50
Birmingham, Alabama 35243
hoffmanmedia.com

ISBN # 978-1-940772-20-2
Printed in China

Cover recipe on page 109
Photography by Marcy Black Simpson

CONTENTS

INTRODUCTION

Bubbling on the stovetop, baking in the oven, or sizzling over a campfire, cast-iron skillets bring back memories of the smells, sights, and sounds of loved ones cooking. When a cast-iron skillet heats up, you know something delicious is on its way. The ingredients can be few—always butter and sugar—and the process can be simple—stir and pour—but like a cauldron made of the same material, a cast-iron skillet produces something magical.

One of the most desired qualities of a cooking utensil is versatility, and the cast-iron skillet is beyond compare in this aspect. Whether you're looking forward to a rich chocolate cake or a seasonal fruit pie, cast-iron skillets deliver. Dearer to us than its performance, however, is the fact that cast iron honors our traditions and the great cooks in our families. Cast iron is often passed down from one generation to the next, and having an heirloom skillet is an honor bestowed on one who is expected to uphold the history baked into its finish.

Whenever you bake in your treasured cast-iron skillets, you remember family and time spent together in the kitchen: peeling peaches for a sweet summer cobbler; standing on a stool as your grandmother instructs you in the fine art of licking a batter-coated spoon; watching a cake rise in the oven and having faith that your well-seasoned skillet will give you a perfect result when you unveil an upside down cake's ooey-gooey goodness.

One thing we know for certain: our stoves and tabletops wouldn't be complete without these familiar black skillets filled with sweet and bubbling cobblers, pies, and crisps. This collection of decadent desserts will remind you of simpler times and help you carry traditions forward. With chocolate indulgences, fall harvest favorites, summer fruit crisps and cobblers, citrus and spice cakes, and pecan delights, this collection of recipes shares more than skillets full of sweets— it shares a heaping serving of love.

Chocolate INDULGENCES

DARK, DECADENT CHOCOLATE MELTS INTO OUR
MOST CRAVEWORTHY SKILLET DESSERTS.

CHOCOLATE FUDGE CAKE

Yield: approximately 12 servings

½ cup hot water
3 ounces unsweetened chocolate, chopped
1 tablespoon instant coffee
½ cup unsalted butter, softened
2 cups sugar
2 large eggs
1 teaspoon vanilla extract
2 cups cake flour, such as Swans Down
1 teaspoon baking powder
1 cup sour cream
8 ounces semisweet chocolate, chopped
½ cup heavy whipping cream

Preheat oven to 350°.

In a medium bowl, stir together ½ cup hot water, unsweetened chocolate, and coffee until smooth. Set aside.

In a large bowl, beat butter and sugar at high speed with a mixer until fluffy, 3 to 4 minutes, stopping to scrape sides of bowl. Add eggs and vanilla, beating to combine. Stir in melted chocolate mixture. Add flour, baking powder, and sour cream; beat just until combined. Pour batter into a 12-inch cast-iron skillet.

In a microwave-safe bowl, microwave semisweet chocolate and cream 1 minute. Let stand 5 minutes; whisk until smooth. Pour melted chocolate over batter in skillet; swirl using the tip of a knife.

Bake until sides pull away from pan, approximately 30 minutes. Serve warm from skillet.

CHOCOLATE-PEANUT BUTTER-BANANA UPSIDE DOWN CAKE

Yield: 1 (10-inch) cake

Topping:
½ cup unsalted butter
¾ cup firmly packed light brown sugar
¼ cup creamy peanut butter
1 tablespoon water
1 teaspoon vanilla extract
4 bananas, sliced ¼ inch thick

Cake:
½ cup unsalted butter
1 cup sugar
1 large egg
¾ cup creamy peanut butter
1¼ cups all-purpose flour
¼ cup unsweetened cocoa powder
1 teaspoon baking powder
½ teaspoon baking soda
½ teaspoon kosher salt
½ cup whole milk
1 teaspoon vanilla extract

Preheat oven to 350°.

FOR TOPPING:

In a 10-inch cast-iron skillet, melt butter over medium heat. Stir in brown sugar and peanut butter until smooth. Bring to a boil; stir in 1 tablespoon water and vanilla until combined. Cook 1 minute more. Remove from heat. Arrange banana slices over caramel. Set aside.

FOR CAKE:

In a large bowl, beat butter and sugar at medium speed with a mixer until fluffy, 3 to 4 minutes, stopping to scrape sides of bowl. Add egg and peanut butter, beating to combine.

In a medium bowl, stir together flour, cocoa, baking powder, baking soda, and salt. With mixer on low speed, add flour mixture to butter mixture in thirds, alternating with milk, beginning and ending with flour mixture. Beat in vanilla until combined. Spoon batter over banana in skillet, smoothing top with an offset spatula.

Bake until a wooden pick inserted in center comes out clean, approximately 40 minutes. Let cool in pan 10 minutes. Carefully invert onto a flat serving plate.

CHOCOLATE COBBLER

Yield: approximately 8 servings

1¼ cups sugar, divided
1   cup all-purpose flour
7   tablespoons unsweetened cocoa powder, divided
2   teaspoons baking powder
¼   teaspoon salt
½   cup whole milk
⅓   cup unsalted butter, melted
1½ teaspoons vanilla extract
½   cup firmly packed light brown sugar
1½ cups hot water
Vanilla ice cream, to serve

Preheat oven to 350°.

In a large bowl, stir together ¾ cup sugar, flour, 3 tablespoons cocoa, baking powder, and salt. Stir in milk, melted butter, and vanilla until smooth. Pour batter into a deep 10-inch cast-iron skillet.

Stir together remaining ½ cup sugar, brown sugar, and remaining 4 tablespoons cocoa. Sprinkle cocoa mixture evenly over batter. Pour 1½ cups hot water evenly over top. (Do not stir.)

Bake until center is almost set, 35 to 40 minutes. Let stand 15 minutes.

Spoon into individual dessert dishes. Spoon sauce from bottom of skillet over each serving. Serve with ice cream.

SKILLET S'MORES

Yield: 6 to 8 servings

12 (1-ounce) squares semisweet baking chocolate, chopped

4 cups miniature marshmallows

Graham crackers

Preheat oven to 450°.

In a 10-inch cast-iron skillet, add chocolate in an even layer. Sprinkle marshmallows over chocolate.

Bake until marshmallows are browned and chocolate is melted, 4 to 5 minutes. Let stand 5 minutes before serving. Serve with graham crackers.

Campfire Method

Assemble s'mores as directed; broil until marshmallows are toasted, 1 to 2 minutes.

Place skillet on a grill rack 3 to 4 inches above medium-hot coals. Cook until chocolate melts, 5 to 10 minutes.

CHOCOLATE-PEANUT BUTTER SWIRL SKILLET CAKE

Yield: 8 to 10 servings

1   cup plus 2 tablespoons unsalted butter, softened and divided
2   cups sugar
1   tablespoon vanilla extract
4   large eggs
1¾ cups all-purpose flour
½   teaspoon baking powder
½   teaspoon salt
¾   cup heavy whipping cream
¼   cup unsweetened cocoa powder
1   (4-ounce) bar bittersweet chocolate, melted
½   cup creamy peanut butter

Preheat oven to 350°. In a 12-inch cast-iron skillet, place 2 tablespoons butter. Place skillet in oven to preheat.

In a large bowl, beat remaining 1 cup butter, sugar, and vanilla at medium speed with a mixer until fluffy, 3 to 4 minutes, stopping to scrape sides of bowl. Add eggs, one at a time, beating well after each addition.

In a small bowl, whisk together flour, baking powder, and salt. Gradually add flour mixture to butter mixture, alternating with cream, beginning and ending with flour mixture, beating just until combined after each addition. Reserve ½ cup batter in a small bowl.

Stir cocoa and melted chocolate into remaining batter until smooth. Carefully remove skillet from oven; spoon batter into skillet.

Stir together peanut butter and reserved ½ cup batter until smooth. Drop by tablespoonfuls over chocolate batter in skillet; swirl using the tip of a knife.

Bake until a wooden pick inserted in center comes out clean, 35 to 45 minutes. Let cool completely in skillet.

Humbly delicious, this easy skillet cookie is the perfect weeknight dessert.

CHOCOLATE-PECAN SNICKERDOODLE SKILLET COOKIE

Yield: approximately 8 servings

1   (17.9-ounce) package snickerdoodle
    cookie mix, such as Betty Crocker
1   cup toasted pecans, chopped and divided
1   cup miniature semisweet chocolate
    morsels
Vanilla ice cream, to serve

Preheat oven to 375°.

Prepare cookie mix according to package directions, stirring in ½ cup pecans. Spoon dough into a 10-inch cast-iron skillet; press in an even layer.

Bake until puffed and golden brown, approximately 17 minutes.

Transfer to a wire rack. Immediately sprinkle with chocolate. Let stand until chocolate begins to melt, approximately 5 minutes. Using the back of a spoon, gently spread melted chocolate over cookie. Sprinkle with remaining ½ cup pecans. Let stand until cookie has cooled and chocolate is set, approximately 2 hours. Cut into wedges. Serve with ice cream, if desired.

NUTELLA-SWIRLED BLONDIES

Yield: 8 servings

¾ cup firmly packed light brown sugar
½ cup unsalted butter, melted
1 large egg, lightly beaten
½ teaspoon vanilla extract
1 cup all-purpose flour
½ teaspoon baking powder
½ teaspoon kosher salt
8 teaspoons chocolate-hazelnut spread, such as Nutella

Preheat oven to 350°. Spray a 9-inch cast-iron wedge pan with nonstick cooking spray. Set aside.

In a medium bowl, whisk together brown sugar, melted butter, egg, and vanilla until smooth. In another medium bowl, whisk together flour, baking powder, and salt.

Gradually add egg mixture to flour mixture, stirring to combine. Divide batter evenly among wells in prepared pan. Place 1 teaspoon chocolate-hazelnut spread in each well. Using the tip of a knife, swirl batter.

Bake until golden brown and set, 15 to 18 minutes. Let cool in pan.

Recipe Tip | To create the perfect swirl, move the tip of your knife in a gentle back-and-forth motion.

FLOURLESS CHOCOLATE CAKE

Yield: approximately 6 servings

4   ounces bittersweet chocolate, chopped
4   ounces semisweet chocolate, chopped
¾   cup unsalted butter, cubed
1⅓ cups sugar
4   large eggs
¾   cup unsweetened cocoa powder, sifted
Garnish: sweetened whipped cream, cocoa
     powder

Preheat oven to 375°. Spray an 8-inch cast-iron skillet with nonstick baking spray with flour. Line bottom of pan with parchment paper; spray with nonstick baking spray with flour. Set aside.

In a medium heat-proof bowl, combine chocolates and butter. Set bowl over a pan of simmering water, being careful not to let bottom of bowl touch water. Cook over low heat, whisking frequently, until melted. Remove from heat. Add sugar and eggs, whisking until well combined. Whisk in cocoa. Pour batter into prepared skillet.

Bake until a thin crust forms on top, 25 to 30 minutes. Let cool in skillet 10 minutes. Carefully invert cake onto a flat serving platter. Top with whipped cream, and sprinkle with cocoa, if desired.

UPSIDE DOWN CHOCOLATE-APRICOT CAKE

Yield: approximately 6 servings

12 tablespoons unsalted butter, divided
¾ cup firmly packed light brown sugar
3 teaspoons vanilla extract, divided
2 (15-ounce) cans unpeeled apricot halves in syrup, drained
1 cup sugar
2 large eggs
1 cup all-purpose flour
⅓ cup unsweetened cocoa powder
2 teaspoons baking powder
1 teaspoon kosher salt
1 cup sour cream

Preheat oven to 350°.

In a deep 10-inch cast-iron skillet, melt 4 tablespoons butter over medium heat. Sprinkle brown sugar over melted butter. Cook, without stirring, until mixture comes to a boil, approximately 4 minutes. Remove from heat; stir in 1 teaspoon vanilla. Place apricots, cut side down, over sugar mixture.

In a large bowl, beat remaining 8 tablespoons butter and sugar at medium speed with a mixer until fluffy, 3 to 4 minutes, stopping to scrape sides of bowl. Add eggs, one at a time, beating well after each addition.

In a medium bowl, stir together flour, cocoa, baking powder, and salt. With mixer on low speed, add flour mixture to butter mixture in thirds, alternating with sour cream, beginning and ending with flour mixture. Add remaining 2 teaspoons vanilla, beating until combined. Pour batter over apricots in skillet. Place skillet on a rimmed baking sheet.

Bake until a wooden pick inserted in center comes out clean, 40 to 45 minutes. Let cool in skillet 10 minutes. Carefully invert cake onto a flat serving platter. Serve warm.

CHOCOLATE-BUTTERSCOTCH SKILLET BROWNIES

Yield: 10 to 12 servings

1   cup plus 2 tablespoons unsalted butter
4   ounces unsweetened chocolate, chopped
2   cups sugar
1½   cups firmly packed light brown sugar
5   large eggs
1   tablespoon vanilla extract
1⅔   cups all-purpose flour
⅛   teaspoon kosher salt
1   cup butterscotch morsels
1   cup semisweet chocolate morsels
1   cup toasted pecans, chopped
Vanilla ice cream, to serve

Preheat oven to 350°. In a 12-inch cast-iron skillet, place 2 tablespoons butter. Place skillet in oven to preheat.

In a small saucepan, melt remaining 1 cup butter and unsweetened chocolate over medium-low heat, stirring until smooth. Let cool slightly.

In a large bowl, beat sugars, eggs, and vanilla at medium-high speed with a mixer until fluffy and pale. Reduce speed to medium-low; gradually beat in flour and salt until combined. Stir in melted chocolate mixture until smooth. Stir in butterscotch, chocolate morsels, and pecans. Carefully remove skillet from oven; spoon batter into skillet.

Bake until center is set, 35 to 40 minutes. Let cool 30 minutes. Serve with ice cream.

NUTELLA S'MORES SWEET ROLLS

Yield: approximately 10 rolls

Sweet Roll Dough (recipe below)
1   cup chocolate-hazelnut spread, such as Nutella
2   cups miniature marshmallows, divided
1   cup confectioners' sugar
3   tablespoons heavy whipping cream
Garnish: crushed graham crackers

Spray a 10-inch cast-iron skillet with nonstick cooking spray. Set aside.

Prepare Sweet Roll Dough, and let rise according to recipe directions. Lightly punch down dough. On a lightly floured surface, roll dough into a 14x10-inch rectangle.

Spread chocolate-hazelnut spread evenly over dough. Sprinkle with 1½ cups marshmallows. Starting with one long side, roll dough into a log; pinch seam to seal. Slice into 9 or 10 rolls. Place rolls in prepared skillet. Cover, and let rise in a warm draft-free place (85°) until doubled in size, approximately 45 minutes.

Preheat oven to 350°. Bake, uncovered, until golden brown, approximately 30 minutes. Let cool in skillet on a wire rack 30 minutes.

In a medium bowl, stir together confectioners' sugar and cream until smooth. Spread glaze over warm rolls. Sprinkle with remaining ½ cup marshmallows. Garnish with graham crackers, if desired.

Broil, 5 inches from heat, watching carefully, until marshmallows are toasted.

Sweet Roll Dough

Yield: approximately 10 rolls

3½ to 3¾ cups all-purpose flour
1   (¼-ounce) package active dry yeast
½   cup whole milk
½   cup sour cream
6   tablespoons unsalted butter, cubed
⅓   cup sugar
2   teaspoons kosher salt
1   large egg, lightly beaten

In the work bowl of a stand mixer fitted with the paddle attachment, combine flour and yeast.

In a medium saucepan, combine milk, sour cream, butter, sugar, and salt. Cook over medium heat, stirring occasionally, until mixture reads 120° on a candy thermometer. With mixer on low speed, add milk mixture to flour mixture. Add egg. Beat until dough forms. Turn off mixer.

Switch to dough hook attachment. Beat at medium speed until dough is smooth and elastic, approximately 5 minutes. (Dough should pull away from sides of bowl but stick to bottom.)

Spray a large bowl with nonstick cooking spray. Place dough in prepared bowl, turning to coat top. Cover, and let rise in a warm draft-free place (85°) until dough has doubled in size, approximately 1 hour and 30 minutes.

Citrus AND Spice

BRIGHT CITRUS AND EXOTIC SPICES LEND THEIR PERFUME
TO THESE COMFORTING DESSERTS.

BROWNED BUTTER AND ORANGE SKILLET CAKE

Yield: 1 (12-inch) cake

Candied Orange Slices:

2   navel oranges, cut into ⅛-inch-thick
      slices
1¾   cups sugar, divided
1   cup cold water

Cake:

½   cup browned butter, softened
      (see recipe tip)
1   cup firmly packed light brown sugar
1   teaspoon vanilla extract
1   teaspoon orange extract
4   large eggs
1   teaspoon orange zest
¼   cup fresh orange juice
2   cups all-purpose flour
1½   teaspoons baking powder
½   teaspoon baking soda
½   teaspoon salt
¼   cup apple jelly
¼   cup orange liqueur, such as Grand Marnier

FOR CANDIED ORANGE SLICES:

Preheat oven to 250°. Line a rimmed baking sheet with parchment paper; top with a wire rack.

In a large cast-iron skillet, add orange slices and water to cover. Bring to a simmer over medium heat. Cook, without stirring, 6 minutes; drain.

Return orange slices to skillet. Sprinkle with 1 cup sugar. Pour 1 cup cold water over sugar, stirring to combine. Bring to a simmer over medium-low heat; cook 15 minutes. Carefully remove orange slices from sugar water; arrange in a single layer on prepared rack.

Bake 30 minutes. Place remaining ¾ cup sugar in a shallow dish. Dredge orange slices in sugar, turning to coat both sides. Return to rack; let dry at least 2 hours.

FOR CAKE:

Preheat oven to 350°. Spray a 12-inch cast-iron skillet with nonstick baking spray with flour. Set aside.

In a medium bowl, beat browned butter, brown sugar, and extracts at medium-high speed with a mixer until fluffy, 3 to 4 minutes, stopping to scrape sides of bowl. Add eggs, one at a time, beating well after each addition. Add orange zest and juice.

In a separate medium bowl, sift together flour, baking powder, baking soda, and salt. Reduce mixer speed to low; add flour mixture to butter mixture in thirds, beating well after each addition. Add batter to prepared skillet, smoothing top with an offset spatula. Arrange Candied Orange Slices over batter.

Bake until a wooden pick inserted in center comes out clean, 55 to 65 minutes. Let cool in pan 10 minutes.

In a small saucepan, combine apple jelly and liqueur. Cook over medium heat, whisking constantly, until smooth. Brush over cake and oranges. Let cool 1 hour before serving.

Recipe Tip

To make browned butter, heat ¾ cup unsalted butter in a medium stainless steel skillet over medium heat until butter is golden brown and has a nutty aroma, 7 to 8 minutes. Strain through a fine-mesh sieve into a small bowl. Cover and refrigerate 30 to 45 minutes.

CINNAMON-ORANGE YEAST ROLLS

Yield: 1½ dozen rolls

Cinnamon-Orange Rolls:
1 tablespoon active dry yeast
½ cup plus ¼ teaspoon sugar, divided
½ cup warm water (105° to 115°)
1½ cups warm milk (105° to 115°)
¾ cup unsalted butter, softened and divided
¼ cup all-vegetable shortening
2 teaspoons salt
2 teaspoons vanilla extract
2 large eggs
6½ cups bread flour, divided
1 cup firmly packed light brown sugar
1 tablespoon orange zest
2 teaspoons ground cinnamon

Glaze:
2⅔ cups confectioners' sugar
1 teaspoon orange zest
1 tablespoon fresh orange juice
6 to 8 tablespoons heavy whipping cream

FOR CINNAMON-ORANGE ROLLS:

In the bowl of a stand mixer fitted with the paddle attachment, stir together yeast, ¼ teaspoon sugar, and ½ cup warm water. Let stand until foamy, approximately 5 minutes.

Add remaining ½ cup sugar, warm milk, ¼ cup butter, shortening, salt, vanilla, and eggs. Beat at medium speed until combined.

Gradually add 5 cups flour, beating until a thick batter forms. Switch to dough hook attachment. Gradually add remaining 1½ cups flour, beating at low speed until a soft dough forms and pulls away from sides of bowl.

Turn dough out onto a lightly floured surface. Knead until smooth, 3 or 4 times. Place dough in a large bowl coated with nonstick cooking spray, turning to coat top. Loosely cover, and let rise in a warm draft-free place (85°) until doubled in size, approximately 1 hour and 30 minutes. Gently punch dough down; cover, and let stand 5 minutes.

On a lightly floured surface, roll dough into an 18x12-inch rectangle. In a small bowl, stir together brown sugar, zest, and cinnamon. Gently spread remaining ½ cup butter over dough. Sprinkle cinnamon mixture evenly over butter. Starting with one long side, roll dough; pinch seam to seal.

Place roll, seam side down, on a cutting surface. Cut dough into 18 slices, approximately 1 inch thick.

Preheat oven to 350°. Place rolls close together in 2 (9-inch) cast-iron skillets sprayed with nonstick cooking spray.

Bake until golden brown, 25 to 30 minutes. Let cool completely on a wire rack.

FOR GLAZE:

In a medium bowl, whisk together confectioners' sugar, orange zest and juice, and enough cream to make a smooth glaze. Drizzle over Cinnamon-Orange Rolls.

CINNAMON DUTCH BABY

Yield: approximately 6 servings

4   tablespoons unsalted butter,
     melted and divided
3   large eggs, at room temperature
1   large egg white, at room temperature
²/₃ cup whole milk, at room temperature
¼   cup plus 2 tablespoons sugar, divided
¾   cup all-purpose flour
2   teaspoons ground cinnamon, divided
½   teaspoon vanilla extract
¼   teaspoon salt

Preheat oven to 400°. Place a 12-inch cast-iron skillet in oven while it preheats.

In the container of a blender, combine 2 tablespoons melted butter, eggs, egg white, milk, 2 tablespoons sugar, flour, ½ teaspoon cinnamon, vanilla, and salt. Blend on high speed until batter is smooth and frothy, approximately 30 seconds.

Carefully remove skillet from oven; add remaining 2 tablespoons melted butter. Using a pastry brush, spread butter around skillet to coat sides. Pour batter into skillet.

Bake until puffed, approximately 20 minutes. (Do not open oven during baking.)

In a small bowl, stir together remaining ¼ cup sugar and 1½ teaspoons cinnamon. Sprinkle over hot Dutch baby. Serve immediately from skillet.

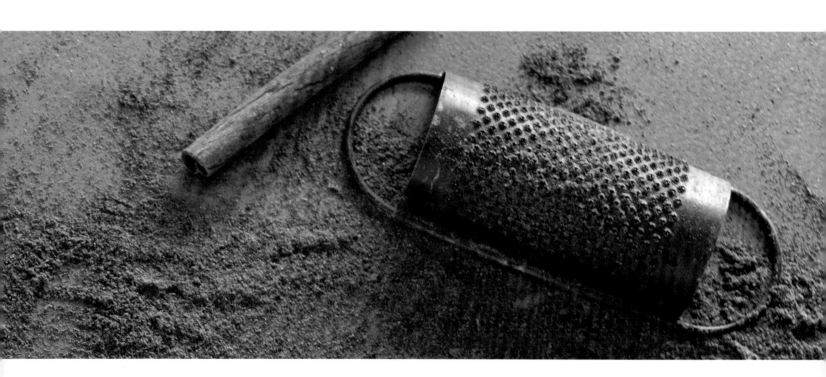

After a dramatic rise, this oven-baked pancake settles into the skillet, yielding a crisp and sweet treat.

SPICED CRUMB CAKE

Yield: 1 (9-inch) cake

Topping:
- ¾ cup all-purpose flour
- ½ cup finely ground almonds
- ¼ cup sugar
- ¼ cup firmly packed light brown sugar
- ¾ teaspoon ground cinnamon
- ½ cup cold unsalted butter, cut into cubes

Cake:
- ½ cup unsalted butter, softened
- ½ cup sugar
- 1 large egg
- ¼ cup sour cream
- 1 teaspoon vanilla extract
- 1½ cups all-purpose flour
- ½ teaspoon ground cinnamon
- ½ teaspoon ground nutmeg
- ½ teaspoon ground ginger
- ½ teaspoon baking soda
- ½ teaspoon salt
- ¼ teaspoon ground cloves
- ½ cup whole buttermilk

Sweetened whipped cream, to serve
Garnish: honey

Preheat oven to 350°. Spray a deep 9-inch cast-iron skillet with nonstick baking spray with flour. Set aside.

FOR TOPPING:

In a medium bowl, stir together flour, almonds, sugars, and cinnamon. Using a fork or pastry blender, cut cold butter into flour mixture until crumbly. Set aside.

FOR CAKE:

In a large bowl, beat butter and sugar at medium-high speed with a mixer until creamy. Add egg, sour cream, and vanilla, beating well.

In another large bowl, stir together flour, cinnamon, nutmeg, ginger, baking soda, salt, and cloves. Gradually add flour mixture to butter mixture in thirds, alternating with buttermilk, beginning and ending with flour mixture. Beat at low speed until well combined. Spoon batter into prepared skillet, smoothing top. Sprinkle topping over batter.

Bake until a wooden pick inserted in center comes out clean, 35 to 40 minutes. Let cool in skillet on a wire rack. Serve with whipped cream. Garnish with honey, if desired.

ORANGE-CARDAMOM BREAKFAST BREAD TWIST

Yield: approximately 10 servings

Dough:
1   (1-pound) package hot roll mix, such as Pillsbury

Filling:
4   tablespoons unsalted butter, softened
½   cup firmly packed light brown sugar
2   teaspoons all-purpose flour
1½ teaspoons orange zest
¾   teaspoon ground cardamom
⅛   teaspoon salt

Glaze:
2   cups confectioners' sugar
¼   cup fresh orange juice

FOR DOUGH:

Prepare mix according to package directions for hot rolls; knead as directed. Cover dough with a large bowl; let stand 5 minutes. On a lightly floured surface, roll dough into a 16x10-inch rectangle.

FOR FILLING:

Spread butter over dough. In a small bowl, stir together brown sugar, flour, zest, cardamom, and salt. Sprinkle sugar mixture over butter; gently press mixture into dough. Starting with one long side, roll dough into a log; pinch seam to seal. Place seam-side down; cut in half lengthwise, stopping 1 inch from end. Twist halves together 3 or 4 times.

Gently place dough in a 12-inch cast-iron skillet, forming a ring. Pinch long ends together to seal. Cover, and let rise in a warm draft-free place (85°) until doubled in size, approximately 40 minutes.

Preheat oven to 375°. Uncover, and bake until golden brown, approximately 25 minutes. Let cool in skillet on a wire rack 30 minutes.

FOR GLAZE:

In a medium bowl, whisk together confectioners' sugar and orange juice; spoon over bread. Let stand 20 minutes before serving.

CAST-IRON SKILLET CINNAMON ROLLS

Yield: approximately 10 rolls

Sweet Roll Dough (recipe below)
½ cup plus 4 tablespoons unsalted butter, softened and divided
¾ cup firmly packed light brown sugar
2 tablespoons ground cinnamon
4 ounces cream cheese, softened
1½ cups confectioners' sugar
4 tablespoons whole milk
½ teaspoon vanilla extract

Spray a 10-inch cast-iron skillet with nonstick cooking spray. Set aside.

Prepare Sweet Roll Dough, and let rise according to recipe directions. Lightly punch down dough. On a lightly floured surface, roll dough into a 14x10-inch rectangle.

Spread ½ cup butter evenly over dough. In a small bowl, stir together brown sugar and cinnamon. Sprinkle over butter. Starting with one long side, roll dough into a log; pinch seam to seal. Slice into 9 or 10 rolls. Place rolls in prepared skillet. Cover, and let rise in a warm draft-free place (85°) until doubled in size, approximately 45 minutes.

Preheat oven to 350°. Bake, uncovered, until golden brown, approximately 30 minutes. Let cool in skillet on a wire rack 30 minutes.

In a medium bowl, beat remaining 4 tablespoons butter and cream cheese at medium speed with a mixer until smooth. Add confectioners' sugar, milk, and vanilla, beating until smooth. Spread glaze over warm rolls.

Sweet Roll Dough

Yield: approximately 10 rolls

3½ to 3¾ cups all-purpose flour
1 (¼-ounce) package active dry yeast
½ cup whole milk
½ cup sour cream
6 tablespoons unsalted butter, cubed
⅓ cup sugar
2 teaspoons kosher salt
1 large egg, lightly beaten

In the work bowl of a stand mixer fitted with the paddle attachment, combine flour and yeast.

In a medium saucepan, combine milk, sour cream, butter, sugar, and salt. Cook over medium heat, stirring occasionally, until mixture reads 120° on a candy thermometer. With mixer on low speed, add milk mixture to flour mixture. Add egg. Beat until dough forms. Turn off mixer.

Switch to dough hook attachment. Beat at medium speed until dough is smooth and elastic, approximately 5 minutes. (Dough should pull away from sides of bowl but stick to bottom.)

Spray a large bowl with nonstick cooking spray. Place dough in prepared bowl, turning to coat top. Cover, and let rise in a warm draft-free place (85°) until dough has doubled in size, approximately 1 hour and 30 minutes.

CITRUS UPSIDE DOWN CAKE

Yield: 1 (10-inch) cake

6   tablespoons unsalted butter
¾   cup firmly packed light brown sugar
1   grapefruit, peeled and thinly sliced
1   orange, peeled and thinly sliced
½   lemon, thinly sliced
2   (8.5-ounce) packages corn muffin mix,
        such as Jiffy
¼   cup sugar
2   large eggs
⅔   cup whole buttermilk
½   teaspoon orange zest

Preheat oven to 350°.

In a 10-inch cast-iron skillet, melt butter over medium heat. Remove from heat. Sprinkle brown sugar over melted butter. Arrange citrus slices over brown sugar in skillet. Set aside.

In a large bowl, whisk together corn muffin mix, sugar, eggs, buttermilk, and zest until well combined. Pour batter over citrus slices.

Bake until a wooden pick inserted in center comes out clean, approximately 35 minutes. Let cool in pan 10 minutes. Carefully invert onto a flat serving plate.

SKILLET APPLE STREUSEL CAKES

Yield: 6 servings

5   tablespoons unsalted butter, softened and divided
6   tablespoons all-purpose flour
6   tablespoons old-fashioned oats
⅓   cup firmly packed dark brown sugar
¾   teaspoon ground cinnamon, divided
1   (9-ounce) package golden yellow cake mix, such as Jiffy
3   cups chopped Granny Smith apple
1   cup confectioners' sugar
4   teaspoons whole milk

Preheat oven to 350°. Lightly grease 6 (5-inch) cast-iron skillets with 1 tablespoon butter. Place prepared skillets on a rimmed baking sheet. Set aside.

In a medium bowl, stir together flour, oats, brown sugar, and ½ teaspoon cinnamon. Add remaining 4 tablespoons butter, combining with fingertips until crumbly.

Prepare cake mix according to package directions, adding remaining ¼ teaspoon cinnamon to batter. Divide batter evenly among prepared skillets. Top each with ½ cup apple. Sprinkle oat mixture evenly over apple.

Bake until lightly browned, 15 to 18 minutes. Let cool completely on a wire rack.

In a small bowl, stir together confectioners' sugar and milk. Drizzle over cakes.

ORANGE SWEET ROLLS

Yield: approximately 10 rolls

Sweet Roll Dough (recipe below)
6 tablespoons unsalted butter, softened
¾ cup sugar
2 tablespoons plus 1 teaspoon orange zest, divided
2 cups confectioners' sugar
4 tablespoons fresh orange juice

Spray a 10-inch cast-iron skillet with nonstick cooking spray. Set aside.

Prepare Sweet Roll Dough, and let rise according to recipe directions. Lightly punch down dough. On a lightly floured surface, roll dough into a 14x10-inch rectangle.

Spread butter evenly over dough. In a small bowl, stir together sugar and 2 tablespoons zest. Sprinkle over butter. Starting with one long side, roll dough into a log; pinch seam to seal. Slice into 9 or 10 rolls. Place rolls in prepared skillet. Cover, and let rise in a warm draft-free place (85°) until doubled in size, approximately 45 minutes.

Preheat oven to 350°. Bake, uncovered, until golden brown, approximately 30 minutes. Let cool in skillet on a wire rack 30 minutes.

In a medium bowl, stir together remaining 1 teaspoon zest, confectioners' sugar, and orange juice until smooth. Drizzle glaze over warm rolls.

Sweet Roll Dough

Yield: approximately 10 rolls

3½ to 3¾ cups all-purpose flour
1 (¼-ounce) package active dry yeast
½ cup whole milk
½ cup sour cream
6 tablespoons unsalted butter, cubed
⅓ cup sugar
2 teaspoons kosher salt
1 large egg, lightly beaten

In the work bowl of a stand mixer fitted with the paddle attachment, combine flour and yeast.

In a medium saucepan, combine milk, sour cream, butter, sugar, and salt. Cook over medium heat, stirring occasionally, until mixture reads 120° on a candy thermometer. With mixer on low speed, add milk mixture to flour mixture. Add egg. Beat until dough forms. Turn off mixer.

Switch to dough hook attachment. Beat at medium speed until dough is smooth and elastic, approximately 5 minutes. (Dough should pull away from sides of bowl but stick to bottom.)

Spray a large bowl with nonstick cooking spray. Place dough in prepared bowl, turning to coat top. Cover, and let rise in a warm draft-free place (85°) until dough has doubled in size, approximately 1 hour and 30 minutes.

Summer
CLASSICS

THE SEASON'S BEST BERRIES AND FRUIT FILL THESE
DESSERTS WITH FRESH-PICKED FLAVOR.

BLUEBERRY-CORNMEAL SKILLET CAKE

Yield: 6 to 8 servings

1¼ cups all-purpose flour
¾ cup plus 1 tablespoon sugar, divided
⅓ cup plain yellow cornmeal
1½ teaspoons kosher salt
1 teaspoon baking powder
½ teaspoon baking soda
½ teaspoon lemon zest
9 tablespoons unsalted butter, divided
1 cup sour cream
2 large eggs
1 teaspoon vanilla extract
2 cups fresh blueberries, divided

Preheat oven to 350°. Place a 10-inch cast-iron skillet in oven to preheat.

In a large bowl, stir together flour, ¾ cup sugar, cornmeal, salt, baking powder, baking soda, and zest. Set aside.

In a medium microwave-safe bowl, microwave 8 tablespoons butter in 30-second intervals until melted. Stir in sour cream, eggs, and vanilla. Make a well in center of dry ingredients. Add butter mixture, stirring to combine.

Carefully remove hot skillet from oven. Melt remaining 1 tablespoon butter in skillet. Add half of batter to pan, spreading in an even layer. Sprinkle 1 cup blueberries evenly over batter. Drop spoonfuls of remaining batter over blueberries. Sprinkle with remaining 1 cup blueberries and remaining 1 tablespoon sugar.

Bake until a wooden pick inserted in center comes out clean, 35 to 40 minutes. Let cool on a wire rack 30 minutes.

PINEAPPLE COBBLER

Yield: approximately 8 servings

5 cups cubed fresh pineapple
8 tablespoons unsalted butter, melted and divided
¼ cup sugar
2 tablespoons all-purpose flour
1 tablespoon lime zest
1 tablespoon fresh lime juice
1½ cups old-fashioned oats
1¼ cups sweetened flaked coconut
½ cup chopped macadamia nuts
½ teaspoon salt
Coconut ice cream, to serve

Preheat oven to 425°.

In a large bowl, stir together pineapple, 2 tablespoons melted butter, sugar, flour, and lime zest and juice. Pour into a deep 9-inch cast-iron skillet.

In a medium bowl, stir together oats, coconut, nuts, salt, and remaining 6 tablespoons melted butter. Sprinkle over pineapple mixture.

Bake until browned and bubbly, 20 to 30 minutes. Serve with coconut ice cream.

PEACH-BLUEBERRY SKILLET COBBLER

Yield: 8 to 10 servings

Topping:
1¼ cups all-purpose flour
½   cup sugar
1½ teaspoons baking powder
1   teaspoon kosher salt
6   tablespoons cold unsalted butter, cubed
½   cup heavy whipping cream
½   cup sliced almonds

Cobbler:
8   cups peeled, pitted, and sliced fresh
    peaches
1   cup fresh blueberries
1   cup firmly packed light brown sugar
2   tablespoons orange zest
1   tablespoon almond extract
2   teaspoons cornstarch
2   tablespoons water
1   tablespoon sparkling sugar

FOR TOPPING:

In a large bowl, stir together flour, sugar, baking powder, and salt. Using a fork or pastry blender, cut butter into flour until mixture resembles coarse crumbs. Stir in cream and almonds just until combined. (Mixture will be crumbly.)

Gently shape dough into a disk. Cover with plastic wrap and refrigerate until ready to use, at least 30 minutes.

FOR COBBLER:

Preheat oven to 375°. In a 12-inch cast-iron skillet, combine peaches, blueberries, brown sugar, zest, and extract. Cook over medium-high heat, stirring occasionally, 8 to 10 minutes. In a small bowl, stir together cornstarch and 2 tablespoons water; stir into peach mixture. Cook, stirring frequently, until thickened, 2 minutes more. Remove from heat.

Divide dough into 8 rounds. Place over fruit mixture; sprinkle with sparkling sugar.

Bake until browned and bubbly, approximately 30 minutes.

SUMMER FRUIT CRISPS

Yield: 4 to 6 servings

½ cup plus 2 tablespoons all-purpose flour, divided
½ cup graham cracker crumbs
½ cup old-fashioned oats
¼ cup unsalted butter, chilled
¼ cup firmly packed light brown sugar
⅛ teaspoon ground cinnamon
⅛ teaspoon ground nutmeg
¼ teaspoon salt
4 fresh peaches, peeled, pitted, and sliced
2 pints fresh blackberries
1 teaspoon vanilla extract
⅓ cup sugar
1 teaspoon cornstarch
Vanilla ice cream, to serve

Preheat oven to 400°. Lightly spray 4 to 6 (8-ounce) cast-iron baking dishes with nonstick cooking spray. Set aside.

In the work bowl of a food processor, pulse together ½ cup flour, graham cracker crumbs, oats, butter, brown sugar, cinnamon, nutmeg, and salt until crumbly. Set aside.

In a medium bowl, stir together peaches, blackberries, and vanilla. In a small bowl, combine sugar, remaining 2 tablespoons flour, and cornstarch. Sprinkle sugar mixture over fruit, stirring to combine. Let stand 10 minutes.

Divide fruit among prepared dishes. Sprinkle with oat mixture.

Bake 12 minutes; cover with foil. Bake 12 minutes more. Let cool on a wire rack 15 minutes. Serve with ice cream.

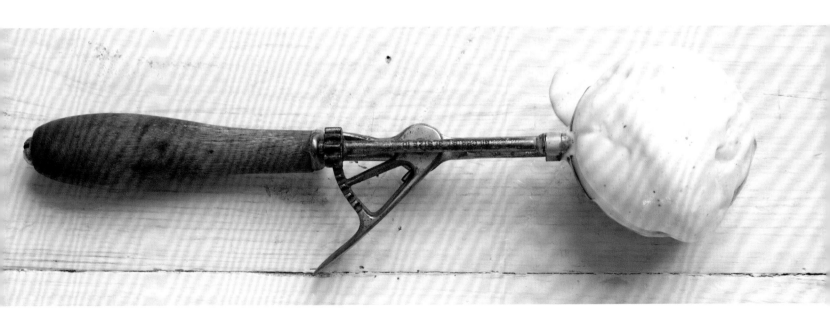

BLACKBERRY-ALMOND UPSIDE DOWN CAKE

Yield: 8 to 10 servings

½ cup unsalted butter, softened
1 cup plus 2 tablespoons sugar
3 large eggs
½ teaspoon almond extract
1½ cups cake flour, such as Swans Down
1 teaspoon baking powder
¼ teaspoon salt
½ cup plus 2 tablespoons whole buttermilk
1⅓ cups sliced toasted almonds, divided
½ cup unsalted butter, melted and divided
1¼ cups firmly packed light brown sugar, divided
3 to 4 cups fresh blackberries

Preheat oven to 350°. Spray a deep 9-inch cast-iron skillet with nonstick cooking spray. Set aside.

In a large bowl, beat butter at medium speed with a mixer until creamy. Gradually add sugar, beating until fluffy, 2 to 4 minutes, stopping to scrape sides of bowl. Add eggs, one at a time, beating well after each addition. Add extract, beating to combine.

In a medium bowl, stir together flour, baking powder, and salt. With mixer on low speed, add flour mixture to butter mixture in thirds, alternating with buttermilk, beginning and ending with flour mixture. Fold in ⅔ cup almonds.

Pour ¼ cup melted butter into prepared skillet. Sprinkle evenly with ¾ cup brown sugar. Arrange blackberries in a single layer over brown sugar. Pour batter over blackberries, smoothing top with an offset spatula.

Bake until a wooden pick inserted in center comes out clean, 40 to 45 minutes. Let cool in skillet 10 minutes. Run a knife around edges to loosen; carefully invert onto a flat serving plate.

In a medium bowl, stir together remaining ¼ cup melted butter, remaining ⅔ cup sliced almonds, and remaining ½ cup brown sugar. Sprinkle over top of cake.

SWEET ROLLS WITH CHERRY PRESERVES

Yield: approximately 10 rolls

Sweet Roll Dough (recipe follows)
1   cup cherry preserves, such as Smucker's
1   teaspoon lemon zest
1½ cups confectioners' sugar
½   cup heavy whipping cream

Spray a 10-inch cast-iron skillet with nonstick cooking spray. Set aside.

Prepare Sweet Roll Dough, and let rise according to recipe directions. Lightly punch down dough. On a lightly floured surface, roll dough into a 14x10-inch rectangle.

Spread preserves evenly over dough; sprinkle with zest. Starting with one long side, roll dough into a log; pinch seam to seal. Slice into 9 or 10 rolls. Place rolls in prepared skillet. Cover, and let rise in a warm draft-free place (85°) until doubled in size, approximately 45 minutes.

Preheat oven to 350°. Bake, uncovered, until golden brown, approximately 30 minutes. Let cool in skillet on a wire rack 30 minutes.

In a medium bowl, stir together confectioners' sugar and cream until smooth. Drizzle glaze over warm rolls.

Sweet Roll Dough

Yield: approximately 10 rolls

3½ to 3¾ cups all-purpose flour
1   (¼-ounce) package active dry yeast
½   cup whole milk
½   cup sour cream
6   tablespoons unsalted butter, cubed
⅓   cup sugar
2   teaspoons kosher salt
1   large egg, lightly beaten

In the work bowl of a stand mixer fitted with the paddle attachment, combine flour and yeast.

In a medium saucepan, combine milk, sour cream, butter, sugar, and salt. Cook over medium heat, stirring occasionally, until mixture reads 120° on a candy thermometer. With mixer on low speed, add milk mixture to flour mixture. Add egg. Beat until dough forms. Turn off mixer.

Switch to dough hook attachment. Beat at medium speed until dough is smooth and elastic, approximately 5 minutes. (Dough should pull away from sides of bowl but stick to bottom.)

Spray a large bowl with nonstick cooking spray. Place dough in prepared bowl, turning to coat top. Cover, and let rise in a warm draft-free place (85°) until dough has doubled in size, approximately 1 hour and 30 minutes.

PEACH SKILLET PIE

Yield: 8 to 10 servings

½   **cup sugar**
¼   **cup firmly packed light brown sugar**
¼   **cup cornstarch**
20 **ripe peaches, peeled, pitted, and sliced**
1½ **(14.1-ounce) packages refrigerated**
     piecrusts (3 sheets), divided
1   **tablespoon heavy whipping cream**

Preheat oven to 350°.

In a large bowl, stir together sugars and cornstarch. Add peaches, stirring to combine.

On a lightly floured surface, stack 2 piecrusts. Roll into a 16-inch circle. Press into bottom and up sides of a deep 10-inch cast-iron skillet. Spoon peach mixture into prepared piecrust.

Roll remaining piecrust into a 12-inch circle. Using a paring knife, cut leaf shapes from dough, discarding cutouts. Place piecrust over peaches; trim to within 1 inch of edges of skillet. Press edges together to seal; fold under, and crimp as desired. Brush top with cream. Place skillet on a rimmed baking sheet.

Bake 45 minutes. Loosely cover with foil, and bake until hot and bubbly, 30 to 45 minutes more.

STRAWBERRY UPSIDE DOWN CAKE

Yield: 1 (10-inch) cake

½   **cup plus 6 tablespoons unsalted butter, softened and divided**
¾   **cup firmly packed light brown sugar**
1   **pint fresh strawberries, halved**
¾   **cup sugar**
1   **large egg**
1½   **cups all-purpose flour**
1   **teaspoon baking powder**
¼   **teaspoon baking soda**
¼   **teaspoon kosher salt**
⅔   **cup whole buttermilk**
½   **teaspoon almond extract**

Preheat oven to 350°.

In a 10-inch cast-iron skillet, melt 6 tablespoons butter over medium heat. Remove from heat. Sprinkle brown sugar over melted butter. Place strawberries cut side down in skillet. Set aside.

In a large bowl, beat remaining ½ cup butter and sugar at medium speed with a mixer until fluffy, 3 to 4 minutes, stopping to scrape sides of bowl. Add egg, beating to combine.

In a medium bowl, stir together flour, baking powder, baking soda, and salt. With mixer on low speed, add flour mixture to butter mixture in thirds, alternating with buttermilk, beginning and ending with flour mixture. Beat in extract until combined. Spoon batter over strawberries, smoothing top with an offset spatula.

Bake until a wooden pick inserted in center comes out clean, approximately 40 minutes. Remove from oven. Let cool in pan 10 minutes. Carefully invert onto a flat serving plate.

BLUEBERRY-RHUBARB CRISP

Yield: 6 to 8 servings

4   cups fresh or frozen sliced rhubarb
3   cups fresh blueberries
¾   cup sugar
¾   cup all-purpose flour, divided
½   teaspoon lemon zest
1   tablespoon fresh lemon juice
1   cup old-fashioned oats
¾   cup firmly packed light brown sugar
½   cup chopped pecans
½   cup unsalted butter, melted
½   teaspoon ground cinnamon

Preheat oven to 350°.

In a large bowl, stir together rhubarb, blueberries, sugar, ¼ cup flour, and lemon zest and juice. Spoon mixture into a 10-inch cast-iron skillet. Set aside.

In a medium bowl, stir together remaining ½ cup flour, oats, brown sugar, pecans, melted butter, and cinnamon. Sprinkle evenly over rhubarb mixture.

Bake until browned and bubby, 35 to 40 minutes. (Loosely cover with foil to prevent excess browning, if necessary.) Let stand 10 minutes before serving.

PINEAPPLE UPSIDE DOWN CAKE

Yield: approximately 8 servings

10 tablespoons unsalted butter, softened
     and divided
2   cups firmly packed light brown sugar,
     divided
2   tablespoons water
1   fresh pineapple, peeled and cored
2   cups cake flour, such as Swans Down
1   teaspoon baking powder
1   teaspoon salt
¾   cup whole milk
2   teaspoons vanilla extract
2   tablespoons spiced rum
2   large eggs

In a 10-inch cast-iron skillet, melt 4 tablespoons butter over medium-low heat. Add ½ cup brown sugar and 2 tablespoons water. Cook, stirring occasionally, 30 minutes. Remove from heat, and let cool 10 minutes.

Cut pineapple into ¼-inch-thick slices; cut slices into quarters. Arrange pineapple in an even layer in skillet. Set aside.

In a medium bowl, whisk together flour, baking powder, and salt. In another bowl, combine milk, vanilla, and rum.

In a large bowl, beat remaining 6 tablespoons butter and remaining 1½ cups brown sugar at medium speed with a mixer until fluffy, 3 to 4 minutes, stopping to scrape sides of bowl. Add eggs, beating to combine. Add flour mixture to butter mixture in thirds, alternating with milk mixture, beating until combined after each addition. Pour batter over pineapple in skillet.

Bake until a wooden pick inserted in center comes out clean, approximately 1 hour. Let cool in skillet 20 minutes. Carefully invert onto a flat serving plate.

STRAWBERRY CRISP

Yield: approximately 6 servings

Filling:
- 5 cups fresh strawberries, halved
- ¼ cup sugar
- 2 tablespoons cornstarch
- ⅛ teaspoon salt
- 1 tablespoon unsalted butter, cut into small pieces

Topping:
- ¾ cup quick-cooking oats
- ⅓ cup firmly packed light brown sugar
- ⅓ cup whole-wheat flour
- ⅓ cup unsalted butter, softened
- ¼ teaspoon salt
- ⅓ cup chopped pecans

Preheat oven to 350°.

FOR FILLING:

In a large bowl, stir together strawberries, sugar, cornstarch, and salt. Spoon mixture into a 10-inch enamel-coated cast-iron skillet; sprinkle with butter.

FOR TOPPING:

In a medium bowl, stir together oats, brown sugar, flour, butter, salt, and pecans until crumbly. Sprinkle over strawberry mixture.

Bake until browned and bubbly, 25 to 30 minutes. Let cool 10 minutes before serving.

Classic rum and brown
sugar-drenched Bananas
Foster gets an update with
this fluffy skillet cake.

BANANAS FOSTER UPSIDE DOWN CAKE

Yield: 10 to 12 servings

1 (15.25 ounce) package yellow cake mix, such as Pillsbury
8 tablespoons unsalted butter
1 cup firmly packed dark brown sugar
¼ cup rum
3 bananas, sliced ¼ inch thick

Preheat oven to 350°.

Prepare cake mix according to package directions. Set aside.

In a 10-inch cast-iron skillet, melt butter over medium-high heat. Remove from heat; stir in brown sugar and rum. Arrange banana slices over brown sugar mixture in skillet. Pour prepared batter over bananas.

Bake until a wooden pick inserted in center comes out clean, 30 to 40 minutes. Let cool in pan 10 minutes. Carefully invert cake onto a flat serving plate. Let cool slightly before serving.

STRAWBERRY-MAPLE COBBLER WITH OATMEAL CRUMBLE

Yield: approximately 4 to 6 servings

Crumble:
- 2 cups quick-cooking oats
- ¾ cup firmly packed light brown sugar
- ½ cup all-purpose flour
- ½ teaspoon ground cinnamon
- ¼ teaspoon salt
- ¾ cup unsalted butter, melted

Cobbler:
- 4 to 6 teaspoons unsalted butter
- 6 cups fresh strawberries, halved
- 1 cup firmly packed light brown sugar
- ¼ cup tapioca flour, sifted
- 1 teaspoon cornstarch
- 2 tablespoons maple syrup
- 2 teaspoons vanilla extract

FOR CRUMBLE:

In a medium bowl, combine oats, brown sugar, flour, cinnamon, and salt. Add melted butter, stirring until combined.

FOR COBBLER:

Preheat oven to 350°. Place 1 teaspoon butter in each of 4 to 6 cast-iron oval mini servers. Place servers in oven until butter melts.

In a large bowl, stir together strawberries, brown sugar, flour, cornstarch, maple syrup, and vanilla. Divide mixture evenly among prepared dishes. Top with crumble.

Bake until browned and bubbly, 25 to 30 minutes. Let cool 5 minutes.

Ripe strawberries melt
into ruby puddles in
these individual crisps.

PEACH AND RASPBERRY CROSTADA

Yield: 6 to 8 servings

Dough:
1¼ cups all-purpose flour
1   teaspoon kosher salt
1   teaspoon sugar
8   tablespoons cold unsalted butter, cubed
3 to 4 tablespoons whole buttermilk, chilled

Filling:
4   cups peeled, pitted, and sliced fresh
    peaches (about 4 peaches)
1½ cups fresh raspberries
½   cup plus 1 tablespoon sugar, divided
¼   cup all-purpose flour
Pinch kosher salt
1   large egg, lightly beaten

Preheat oven to 400°.

FOR DOUGH:

In a medium bowl, stir together flour, salt, and sugar. Using a fork or pastry blender, cut butter into flour mixture until mixture resembles coarse crumbs.

Add buttermilk, 1 tablespoon at a time, stirring until a dough forms. Turn dough out onto a lightly floured surface; shape into a disk. Cover tightly with plastic wrap and refrigerate until firm, at least 30 minutes.

On a lightly floured surface, roll dough into a 12-inch circle. Press into bottom and up sides of a 10-inch cast-iron skillet.

FOR FILLING:

In a large bowl, stir together peaches, raspberries, ½ cup sugar, flour, and salt. Spoon peach mixture into center of pie dough; fold edges over to encase filling. Brush edges with egg, and sprinkle with remaining 1 tablespoon sugar.

Bake on lowest rack 20 minutes. Reduce oven to 350°. Transfer skillet to middle rack. Bake until browned and bubbly, approximately 25 minutes more. (Loosely cover with foil to prevent excess browning, if necessary.)

SKILLET POUND CAKE WITH PEACHES

Yield: approximately 8 servings

Peaches:
- ½ cup sugar
- ½ cup water
- ⅛ teaspoon salt
- 1 tablespoon fresh lemon juice
- ½ teaspoon vanilla extract
- 4 cups peeled, pitted, and sliced fresh peaches

Cake:
- 1 cup unsalted butter, softened
- 1 cup sugar
- 4 large eggs
- 2 cups all-purpose flour
- 1 teaspoon baking powder
- ½ teaspoon salt
- 1 teaspoon vanilla extract
- 2 tablespoons confectioners' sugar
- 2 tablespoons chopped fresh mint

FOR PEACHES:

In a small saucepan, bring sugar, ½ cup water, and salt to a boil over high heat. Cook 1 minute. Remove from heat; stir in lemon juice and vanilla. Transfer to a medium bowl; let cool. Add peaches; cover and refrigerate 2 hours to overnight.

FOR CAKE:

Preheat oven to 325°. In a large bowl, beat butter and sugar at medium speed with a mixer until fluffy, 3 to 4 minutes, stopping to scrape sides of bowl. Add eggs, one at a time, beating well after each addition.

In a medium bowl, whisk together flour, baking powder, and salt. With mixer on low speed, gradually add flour mixture to egg mixture. Beat in vanilla. Spoon batter into a 10-inch cast-iron skillet, smoothing top with an offset spatula.

Bake until a wooden pick inserted in center comes out clean, approximately 35 minutes. Let cool completely on a wire rack. Sprinkle with confectioners' sugar. Stir mint into peach mixture. Serve with pound cake.

BLACKBERRY COBBLER

Yield: approximately 8 servings

6 cups fresh blackberries
1⅓ cups sugar, divided
2 teaspoons lemon zest
2¼ cups all-purpose flour, divided
1¼ teaspoons baking powder
¼ teaspoon kosher salt
¾ cup cold unsalted butter, cubed
¾ cup plus 2 tablespoons whole buttermilk
1 large egg, lightly beaten
2 teaspoons water
2 teaspoons turbinado sugar

Preheat oven to 350°.

In a 12-inch cast-iron skillet, stir together blackberries, 1 cup sugar, and zest over medium heat. Cook, stirring occasionally, until blackberries soften and sugar dissolves, 8 to 10 minutes. Stir in ¼ cup flour until combined. Remove from heat.

In a large bowl, whisk together remaining 2 cups flour, remaining ⅓ cup sugar, baking powder, and salt until combined. Using a fork or pastry blender, cut butter into flour mixture until crumbly. Add buttermilk, stirring until combined. Drop spoonfuls of dough over blackberry mixture.

In a small bowl, whisk together egg and 2 teaspoons water. Brush over dough; sprinkle with turbinado sugar.

Bake until browned and bubbly, approximately 30 minutes. Let cool 15 minutes.

STRAWBERRY POUND CAKE

Yield: 6 to 8 servings

¾   cup plus 2 tablespoons unsalted butter, softened
1½   cups sugar
4   large eggs
1   teaspoon strawberry extract
1¾   cups all-purpose flour
¼   teaspoon kosher salt
⅓   cup sour cream
1   cup sliced fresh strawberries
Garnish: confectioners' sugar

Preheat oven to 350°. In a 10-inch cast-iron skillet, place 2 tablespoons butter. Place skillet in oven to preheat.

In a large bowl, beat remaining ¾ cup butter and sugar at medium speed with a mixer until fluffy, 3 to 4 minutes, stopping to scrape sides of bowl. Add eggs, one at a time, beating well after each addition. Beat in extract. Gradually beat in flour and salt until smooth. Stir in sour cream. Carefully remove skillet from oven; spoon batter into skillet. Top with strawberries.

Bake until a wooden pick inserted in center comes out clean, 30 to 35 minutes. Let cool in skillet 30 minutes. Garnish with confectioners' sugar, if desired.

MINIATURE PEACH COBBLERS

Yield: 6 servings

Topping:
- ⅔ cup all-purpose flour
- ¼ cup sugar
- ¾ teaspoon baking powder
- ½ teaspoon kosher salt
- 3 tablespoons cold unsalted butter, cubed
- ¼ cup plus 1 tablespoon heavy whipping cream, divided

Cobblers:
- 6 cups peeled, pitted, and sliced fresh peaches
- 2 tablespoons fresh orange juice
- 1 tablespoon fresh lemon juice
- 2 tablespoons unsalted butter
- 1 cup sugar
- 2 teaspoons cornstarch
- ½ teaspoon ground cinnamon
- ¼ teaspoon ground nutmeg

FOR TOPPING:

In a large bowl, stir together flour, sugar, baking powder, and salt. Using a fork or pastry blender, cut butter into flour until mixture resembles coarse crumbs. Stir in ¼ cup cream just until combined, adding remaining 1 tablespoon cream, if needed. (Mixture will be crumbly.)

Gently shape dough into a disk. Cover with plastic wrap and refrigerate until ready to use.

FOR COBBLERS:

Preheat oven to 350°. In a large saucepan, cook peaches, orange juice, lemon juice, and butter over medium heat, stirring occasionally, until butter melts, approximately 8 minutes.

In a medium bowl, whisk together sugar, cornstarch, cinnamon, and nutmeg; stir into peach mixture until combined. Remove from heat.

Divide peach mixture among 6 (1½-cup) miniature cast-iron skillets. Divide dough into 6 portions; place over peach mixture in skillets. Place on a rimmed baking sheet.

Bake until browned and bubbly, 25 to 28 minutes.

COCONUT CUSTARD PIE WEDGES

Yield: 8 servings

½ (14.1-ounce) package refrigerated piecrusts (1 sheet)
½ cup sugar
2 tablespoons unsalted butter, melted
3 large eggs
½ cup whole buttermilk
1 teaspoon vanilla extract
1 cup sweetened flaked coconut
Garnish: sweetened whipped cream, toasted coconut

Preheat oven to 350°. Spray a 9-inch cast-iron wedge pan with nonstick cooking spray.

On a lightly floured surface, roll piecrust into a 12-inch circle; cut into 8 equal triangles. Press triangles into bottom and up sides of wells in prepared pan.

In a medium bowl, whisk together sugar, melted butter, and eggs until smooth. Whisk in buttermilk and vanilla. Stir in coconut. Divide batter evenly among wells.

Bake until golden brown and centers are set, approximately 20 minutes. Let cool in pan 1 hour. Garnish with whipped cream and coconut, if desired.

Pecan
DELIGHTS

FROM CLASSIC PIES AND CAKES TO COOKIES AND SWEET ROLLS,
THESE RECIPES CELEBRATE THE SOUTH'S FAVORITE NUT.

OATMEAL-PECAN SKILLET BLONDIE

Yield: 8 to 10 servings

¾   cup unsalted butter, softened
½   cup firmly packed light brown sugar
½   cup sugar
1   tablespoon vanilla extract
2   large eggs
1¾ cups all-purpose flour
½   teaspoon baking soda
½   teaspoon baking powder
¼   teaspoon kosher salt
1½ cups quick-cooking oats
1   cup toasted pecans, chopped

Preheat oven to 350°.

In a large bowl, beat butter, sugars, and vanilla at medium speed with a mixer until fluffy, 3 to 4 minutes, stopping to scrape sides of bowl. Add eggs, one at a time, beating just until combined after each addition.

In a small bowl, whisk together flour, baking soda, baking powder, and salt. Gradually add flour mixture to butter mixture, beating until combined. Beat in oats and pecans. Spoon batter into a deep 10-inch cast-iron skillet.

Bake until center is set, 25 to 35 minutes. Let cool completely.

BUTTERSCOTCH-PECAN PERSONAL PAN COOKIES

Yield: 12 servings

1 cup unsalted butter, softened
1½ cups firmly packed light brown sugar
1 cup sugar
3 large eggs
2 teaspoons vanilla extract
3 cups all-purpose flour
1½ teaspoons baking powder
1½ teaspoons kosher salt
1 (11-ounce) package butterscotch morsels
1 cup chopped pecans
Vanilla ice cream, to serve

Preheat oven to 375°.

In a large bowl, beat butter and sugars at high speed with a mixer until fluffy, 3 to 4 minutes, stopping to scrape sides of bowl. Add eggs, one at a time, beating well after each addition. Beat in vanilla.

In a small bowl, whisk together flour, baking powder, and salt. Reduce mixer speed to low; add flour mixture to butter mixture, beating just until combined. Stir in butterscotch and pecans. Divide dough evenly among 12 (4½-inch) cast-iron skillets, or place in 1 (12-inch) cast-iron skillet.

Bake until lightly browned, approximately 30 minutes. Let cool 10 minutes. Serve in skillets with ice cream.

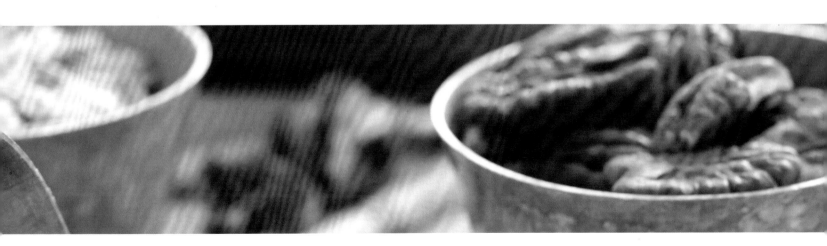

PECAN UPSIDE DOWN CAKE

Yield: approximately 8 servings

Topping:

1   **cup finely chopped pecans**
½   **cup unsalted butter, cut into small pieces**
½   **cup firmly packed dark brown sugar**
¼   **cup light corn syrup**
¼   **teaspoon salt**

Cake:

1⅔   **cups all-purpose flour**
¾   **cup sugar**
1   **teaspoon baking powder**
¾   **teaspoon salt**
½   **teaspoon baking soda**
¾   **cup whole buttermilk**
6   **tablespoons unsalted butter, melted**
1   **teaspoon vanilla extract**
2   **large eggs**
Vanilla ice cream, to serve

Preheat oven to 350°.

FOR TOPPING:

Spray a 10-inch cast-iron skillet with nonstick cooking spray. Add pecans, butter, brown sugar, corn syrup, and salt. Cook over medium heat, stirring occasionally, until smooth, 2 to 3 minutes. Remove from heat.

FOR CAKE:

In a medium bowl, whisk together flour, sugar, baking powder, salt, and baking soda. In another medium bowl, whisk together buttermilk, melted butter, vanilla, and eggs. Add to flour mixture, stirring until smooth. Gently spoon batter over pecan mixture in skillet. (Do not stir.)

Bake until golden brown and a wooden pick inserted in center comes out clean, 20 to 25 minutes. Remove from oven. Let stand in pan 10 minutes. Carefully invert onto a flat serving plate. Spoon any remaining pecan mixture in skillet over cake. Serve with ice cream.

PRALINE CAKE

Yield: approximately 8 servings

Cake:
- ¾ cup unsalted butter, softened and divided
- 1 cup firmly packed light brown sugar
- ¼ cup heavy whipping cream
- 1 cup sugar
- 3 large eggs
- ½ teaspoon vanilla extract
- 1½ cups cake flour, such as Swans Down
- 1 teaspoon baking powder
- ¼ teaspoon salt
- ½ cup plus 2 tablespoons whole buttermilk
- 1 cup chopped pecans
- 1 cup pecan halves

Sauce:
- 1 cup firmly packed light brown sugar
- ¼ cup brandy
- 3 tablespoons water
- 1 tablespoon unsalted butter
- 1 tablespoon light corn syrup
- ⅛ teaspoon salt
- 1 tablespoon heavy whipping cream

Preheat oven to 350°.

FOR CAKE:

In a deep 10-inch cast-iron skillet, melt ¼ cup butter over medium heat. Add brown sugar, stirring until dissolved. Stir in cream until combined. Remove from heat.

In a large bowl, beat remaining ½ cup butter at medium speed with a mixer until creamy. Gradually add sugar, beating until fluffy, 3 to 4 minutes, stopping to scrape sides of bowl. Add eggs, one at a time, beating well after each addition. Beat in vanilla.

In a medium bowl, stir together flour, baking powder, and salt. Add flour mixture to butter mixture in thirds, alternating with buttermilk, beginning and ending with flour mixture. Fold in chopped pecans.

Arrange pecan halves in bottom of skillet as desired. Spoon batter over pecans.

Bake until a wooden pick inserted in center comes out clean, 40 to 45 minutes. Run a knife around the edge of skillet to loosen. Carefully invert cake onto a flat serving plate.

FOR SAUCE:

In a medium saucepan, combine brown sugar, brandy, 3 tablespoons water, butter, corn syrup, and salt. Bring to a boil over medium-high heat, stirring frequently. Reduce heat to medium-low; cook 2 minutes, stirring frequently. Remove from heat; stir in cream. Pour into a small bowl. Let cool 30 minutes. Serve with cake.

PECAN-COCONUT MONKEY BREAD

Yield: approximately 6 servings

1   (16.3-ounce) can refrigerated buttermilk
     biscuits, such as Pillsbury Grands
½   cup unsalted butter, melted
¾   cup sugar
2   teaspoons ground cinnamon
⅓   cup chopped pecans
⅓   cup sweetened flaked coconut
Cane syrup or maple syrup, to serve

Preheat oven to 350°. Spray a 10-inch enamel-coated cast-iron skillet with nonstick cooking spray. Set aside.

Cut biscuits into quarters. In a small bowl, add melted butter. In another small bowl, stir together sugar and cinnamon. Working in batches, dip biscuit pieces in butter; roll in sugar mixture to coat. Place biscuit pieces in prepared skillet. Sprinkle evenly with pecans and coconut.

Bake until golden brown, approximately 25 minutes. Let cool 15 minutes. Drizzle with cane syrup or maple syrup, if desired.

UPSIDE DOWN DOUGHNUT CAKE

Yield: 1 (10-inch) cake

Topping:
½ cup unsalted butter
¾ cup firmly packed light brown sugar
3 tablespoons fresh brewed coffee
¾ cup chopped pecans
5 glazed doughnuts, such as Krispy Kreme
6 doughnut holes, such as Krispy Kreme

Cake:
½ cup unsalted butter
1 cup firmly packed light brown sugar
1 large egg
1⅓ cups all-purpose flour
2 teaspoons baking powder
½ teaspoon kosher salt
⅓ cup whole milk
1 teaspoon vanilla extract

Preheat oven to 350°.

FOR TOPPING:

In a 10-inch cast-iron skillet, melt butter over medium heat. Stir in brown sugar. Bring mixture to a boil; stir in coffee and pecans. Cook 1 minute. Remove from heat. Press doughnuts into bottom of skillet; fill in spaces with doughnut holes. Let cool completely.

FOR CAKE:

In a large bowl, beat butter and brown sugar at medium speed with a mixer until fluffy, 3 to 4 minutes, stopping to scrape sides of bowl. Add egg, beating to combine.

In a medium bowl, stir together flour, baking powder, and salt. With mixer on low speed, add flour mixture to butter mixture in thirds, alternating with milk, beginning and ending with flour mixture. Beat in vanilla until combined. Spoon batter over doughnuts in skillet, smoothing top with an offset spatula.

Bake until a wooden pick inserted in center comes out clean, approximately 40 minutes. Let cool in pan 10 minutes. Carefully invert onto a flat serving plate.

PECAN PIE CRISP

Yield: approximately 6 servings

¾ cup all-purpose flour
¼ cup firmly packed light brown sugar
⅛ teaspoon ground nutmeg
3 tablespoons unsalted butter, softened
¼ cup chopped pecans
1 cup light corn syrup
1 cup sugar
¼ teaspoon salt
2 tablespoons unsalted butter, melted
1 teaspoon vanilla extract
3 large eggs, lightly beaten
2 cups pecan halves
Vanilla ice cream, to serve

Preheat oven to 350°. Spray a 10-inch enamel-coated cast-iron skillet with nonstick cooking spray. Set aside.

In a medium bowl, stir together flour, brown sugar, and nutmeg. Stir in butter and pecans until crumbly. Set aside.

In another medium bowl, whisk together corn syrup, sugar, salt, melted butter, vanilla, and eggs. Place pecan halves in prepared skillet. Pour corn syrup mixture over pecans. Top with crumble mixture.

Bake until filling is bubbly and set, 25 to 30 minutes. Let cool 15 minutes before serving. Serve with ice cream.

Covered in golden caramel and sprinkled with crunchy pecans and coconut, these gooey sweet rolls are a knockout.

COCONUT-PECAN-CARAMEL ROLLS

Yield: approximately 10 rolls

Caramel Topping:
- ³⁄₄ cup firmly packed light brown sugar
- ³⁄₄ cup heavy whipping cream
- ½ cup unsalted butter, cubed
- ⅓ cup cane syrup, such as Steen's
- ¼ teaspoon kosher salt
- ⅔ cup sweetened flaked coconut, toasted and divided
- ⅔ cup pecans, toasted, chopped, and divided

Rolls:
- Sweet Roll Dough (recipe on page 73)
- ½ cup unsalted butter, softened
- ½ cup firmly packed light brown sugar
- ⅓ cup sweetened flaked coconut, toasted
- ⅓ cup toasted pecans, chopped
- 2 teaspoons pumpkin pie spice
- ¼ teaspoon kosher salt

FOR CARAMEL TOPPING:

In a 10-inch cast-iron skillet, bring brown sugar, cream, butter, cane syrup, and salt to a boil over medium heat. Cook, stirring occasionally, until mixture thickens, approximately 5 minutes. Remove from heat. Reserve half of caramel; set aside. Sprinkle ⅓ cup coconut and ⅓ cup pecans over remaining caramel in skillet. Set aside.

FOR ROLLS:

Prepare Sweet Roll Dough, and let rise according to recipe directions. Lightly punch down dough. On a lightly floured surface, roll dough into a 14x10-inch rectangle.

Spread butter evenly over dough. In a small bowl, stir together brown sugar, coconut, pecans, pumpkin pie spice, and salt. Sprinkle evenly over butter. Starting with one long side, roll dough into a log; pinch seam to seal. Slice into 9 or 10 rolls. Place rolls on caramel sauce in skillet. Cover, and let rise in a warm draft-free place (85°) until doubled in size, approximately 45 minutes.

Preheat oven to 350°. Place skillet on a rimmed baking sheet. Bake, uncovered, until golden brown, approximately 35 minutes. Let cool in skillet on a wire rack 30 minutes.

To serve, pour reserved caramel over warm rolls. Sprinkle with remaining ⅓ cup coconut and remaining ⅓ cup pecans.

ORANGE-PECAN PIE

Yield: 6 to 8 servings

1 (14.1-ounce) package refrigerated
piecrusts (2 sheets)
1½ cups firmly packed light brown sugar
1½ cups light corn syrup
⅓ cup unsalted butter, melted
5 large eggs
¼ cup orange-flavored liqueur
1 tablespoon orange zest
2 teaspoons vanilla extract
¼ teaspoon kosher salt
3 cups chopped pecans

Preheat oven to 350°.

On a lightly floured surface, stack 2 piecrusts. Roll into a 16-inch circle. Press into bottom and up sides of a deep 10-inch cast-iron skillet. Trim piecrust to within 1 inch of edges of skillet. Fold edges under, and crimp as desired. Top with a piece of parchment paper, letting ends extend over edges of skillet. Add pie weights.

Bake 10 minutes; remove paper and weights. Set aside.

In a large bowl, stir together brown sugar, corn syrup, melted butter, eggs, liqueur, zest, vanilla, and salt until smooth. Stir in pecans. Spoon mixture into prepared piecrust.

Bake until center is set, 55 minutes to 1 hour and 10 minutes. (Loosely cover with foil halfway through baking to prevent excess browning.) Let cool completely.

Harvest
FAVORITES

FROM APPLES AND PEARS TO SWEET POTATOES AND CRANBERRIES,
THESE SKILLET DESSERTS SING WITH AUTUMN FLAVOR.

CRANBERRY-APPLE UPSIDE DOWN JOHNNYCAKE

Yield: approximately 8 servings

⅓   cup unsalted butter
1   cup firmly packed light brown sugar
1   tablespoon light corn syrup
⅓   cup plus 3 tablespoons apple cider, divided
1½   large Granny Smith apples, peeled and cut into ¼-inch-thick slices
1   teaspoon fresh lemon juice
½   cup sweetened dried cranberries
2   (8.5-ounce) packages corn muffin mix, such as Jiffy
2   large eggs
⅓   cup whole milk

Preheat oven to 350°.

In a deep 10-inch cast-iron skillet, bring butter, brown sugar, and corn syrup to a boil over medium heat, stirring occasionally, approximately 2 minutes. Stir in 3 tablespoons apple cider; cook 1 minute more. Remove from heat; let cool completely.

In a small bowl, stir together apple and lemon juice. Arrange apple in a circle over cooled caramel in skillet, overlapping slightly. Sprinkle with cranberries.

In a medium bowl, stir together corn muffin mix, eggs, milk, and remaining ⅓ cup apple cider until well combined. Pour batter over fruit in skillet, smoothing top with an offset spatula.

Bake until a wooden pick inserted in center comes out clean, 30 to 35 minutes. Let cool in skillet 30 minutes. Run a knife around edges to loosen; carefully invert onto a flat serving plate.

TART APPLE CRISP

Yield: approximately 4 servings

Topping:
- ¾ cup firmly packed light brown sugar
- ½ cup all-purpose flour
- ½ cup old-fashioned oats
- ½ teaspoon ground cinnamon
- ¼ teaspoon ground ginger
- ¼ teaspoon ground cloves
- ⅛ teaspoon salt
- ⅓ cup unsalted butter, softened

Filling:
- 3 Granny Smith apples, peeled and sliced crosswise (about 1½ pounds)
- 2 teaspoons all-purpose flour
- ⅛ teaspoon salt
- ¼ cup apple juice
- 3 tablespoons fresh lemon juice
- 2 tablespoons cold unsalted butter, diced

Preheat oven to 375°.

FOR TOPPING:

In a medium bowl, combine brown sugar, flour, oats, cinnamon, ginger, cloves, and salt; add butter. Combine with fingertips until crumbly.

FOR FILLING:

In a 10-inch cast-iron skillet, place apple; sprinkle with flour and salt. Drizzle with juices, stirring to combine. Sprinkle diced butter over apple mixture. Sprinkle with topping mixture.

Bake until lightly browned and bubbly, approximately 30 minutes. Let stand 10 minutes before serving.

PUMPKIN SPICE SKILLET COOKIE

Yield: approximately 4 servings

½ cup unsalted butter, softened
¾ cup firmly packed light brown sugar
1 large egg
1 teaspoon vanilla extract
¾ cup all-purpose flour
1 teaspoon pumpkin pie spice
¾ teaspoon baking powder
¼ teaspoon kosher salt
½ cup plus 2 tablespoons old-fashioned oats, divided
½ cup sweetened dried cranberries, divided
⅓ cup butterscotch morsels, divided

Preheat oven to 325°. Spray an 8-inch cast-iron skillet with nonstick baking spray with flour. Set aside.

In a large bowl, beat butter and brown sugar at medium speed with a mixer until fluffy, 3 to 4 minutes, stopping to scrape sides of bowl. Add egg and vanilla; beat until combined.

In a small bowl, whisk together flour, pumpkin pie spice, baking powder, and salt. Reduce speed to low; add flour mixture to butter mixture, beating just until combined. Stir in ½ cup oats.

Press half of dough into bottom of skillet. Sprinkle with half of cranberries and half of butterscotch. Top with spoonfuls of remaining dough. Sprinkle with remaining 2 tablespoons oats, remaining cranberries, and remaining butterscotch.

Bake until golden brown, approximately 45 minutes. (Loosely cover with foil to prevent excess browning, if necessary.) Let cool 15 minutes.

Sweet and tart, these
cranberries burst during
baking, lending their warm
ruby glow to this sweet crisp.

CRANBERRY-APPLE CRISP

Yield: approximately 6 servings

½ cup plus 2 tablespoons unsalted butter
4 Pink Lady apples, peeled and thinly sliced
2 cups fresh or frozen cranberries
1½ cups firmly packed light brown sugar, divided
⅓ cup fresh orange juice
½ cup plus 1 tablespoon all-purpose flour, divided
½ teaspoon ground cinnamon
¼ teaspoon ground cardamom
¼ teaspoon ground nutmeg
1 cup old-fashioned oats
½ cup chopped pecans
½ teaspoon kosher salt

Preheat oven to 350°.

In a 12-inch cast-iron skillet, melt butter over medium-high heat. Remove from heat; reserve ½ cup melted butter, and set aside. Add apple, cranberries, ¾ cup brown sugar, orange juice, 1 tablespoon flour, cinnamon, cardamom, and nutmeg to skillet, stirring to combine.

In a medium bowl, stir together oats, remaining ¾ cup brown sugar, pecans, remaining ½ cup flour, reserved ½ cup melted butter, and salt. Sprinkle evenly over apple mixture.

Bake until browned and bubbly, approximately 30 minutes.

SKILLET-TOASTED NUTS WITH FRUIT AND HONEY

Yield: approximately 2 cups

½   cup pecans, roughly chopped
½   cup walnuts, roughly chopped
½   cup roasted salted pistachios
1   cup honey
1   teaspoon orange zest
¼   cup canola oil
¼   cup dried apricots, diced
¼   cup dried tart cherries
¼   teaspoon kosher salt
Vanilla ice cream, to serve

In a medium cast-iron skillet, add pecans, walnuts, and pistachios. Cook over medium heat, stirring frequently, until nuts are lightly toasted and fragrant, approximately 10 minutes. Remove from heat. Set aside.

In a medium bowl, whisk together honey, zest, and canola oil until combined. Add apricots and cherries to toasted nuts in skillet. Add honey mixture and salt, stirring to combine.

Serve warm or at room temperature over ice cream, if desired. Cover and refrigerate up to 1 month.

The mingling of warm
and cool flavors makes
this dessert irresistible.

APPLE STREUSEL PIE

Yield: 1 (10-inch) pie

Dough:
1⅓ cups all-purpose flour
2 teaspoons sugar
½ teaspoon salt
½ cup cold unsalted butter, cubed
3 to 4 tablespoons cold apple cider

Filling:
6 cups sliced apple, such as Gala (about 2½ pounds)
⅓ cup sugar
⅓ cup firmly packed light brown sugar
2 tablespoons cornstarch
1½ teaspoons apple pie spice
⅛ teaspoon salt
1 tablespoon fresh lemon juice

Streusel:
½ cup old-fashioned oats
⅓ cup all-purpose flour
2 tablespoons firmly packed light brown sugar
⅛ teaspoon salt
2 tablespoons unsalted butter, melted

Garnish: prepared caramel sauce

FOR DOUGH:

In the work bowl of a food processor, pulse together flour, sugar, and salt. Add butter, pulsing until mixture resembles coarse crumbs. With processor running, gradually add 3 tablespoons apple cider until a dough forms. (Add remaining 1 tablespoon apple cider, if needed.) Turn dough out onto a lightly floured surface; shape into a disk. Cover with plastic wrap; refrigerate 30 minutes. Remove from refrigerator 15 minutes before rolling.

On a lightly floured surface, roll dough into a 13-inch circle. Transfer to a 10-inch cast-iron skillet, pressing into bottom and up sides. Fold edges under.

Preheat oven to 375°.

FOR FILLING:

In a large bowl, stir together apple, sugars, cornstarch, apple pie spice, and salt. Sprinkle with lemon juice; stir to combine. Spoon apple mixture into prepared piecrust.

FOR STREUSEL:

In a medium bowl, stir together oats, flour, brown sugar, and salt. Add melted butter, stirring until crumbly. Sprinkle over filling.

Bake until crust is golden brown and apples are tender, approximately 45 minutes. (Loosely cover with foil during last 10 minutes to prevent excess browning, if necessary.) Drizzle with caramel, if desired.

UPSIDE DOWN SWEET POTATO CAKE

Yield: 1 (9-inch) cake

¾ cup cane syrup, divided
2   tablespoons unsalted butter
2½ cups peeled thinly sliced sweet potato
1¾ cups self-rising flour
¾ cup sugar
¼ cup whole milk
10 tablespoons unsalted butter, melted
3   large eggs, lightly beaten
¾ cup sour cream

Preheat oven to 350°.

In a 10-inch cast-iron skillet, combine ½ cup cane syrup and 2 tablespoons butter. Bring to a boil over medium heat; cook 1 minute. Remove from heat. Layer sweet potato in bottom of skillet, overlapping slices slightly.

In a large bowl, stir together flour and sugar. Add remaining ¼ cup cane syrup, milk, melted butter, eggs, and sour cream. Beat at low speed with a mixer until smooth. Gently spread over sweet potato.

Bake until set and golden brown, approximately 30 minutes. Let stand 5 minutes. Carefully invert cake onto a flat serving plate.

Studded with candied
pears, this harvest-spiced
cake is sticky and sweet.

UPSIDE DOWN PEAR GINGERBREAD CAKE

Yield: approximately 8 servings

½ cup plus ⅓ cup unsalted butter, softened and divided
1½ cups firmly packed light brown sugar, divided
2 tablespoons water
2 Bosc pears, peeled and thickly sliced
1 large egg
2 cups all-purpose flour
1 teaspoon baking soda
1 teaspoon ground cinnamon
1 teaspoon ground ginger
¾ teaspoon kosher salt
¼ teaspoon ground cloves
¾ cup unsulfured molasses
½ cup boiling water

Preheat oven to 350°.

In a deep 9-inch cast-iron skillet, bring ½ cup butter and 1 cup brown sugar to a boil over medium heat, stirring until mixture pulls away from sides of skillet, 2 to 3 minutes. Stir in 2 tablespoons water; cook 1 minute more. Remove from heat. Arrange pears over sugar mixture in skillet.

In a large bowl, beat remaining ⅓ cup butter, remaining ½ cup brown sugar, and egg at medium speed with a mixer until smooth.

In a medium bowl, stir together flour, baking soda, cinnamon, ginger, salt, and cloves. In another medium bowl, whisk together molasses and ½ cup boiling water until combined.

With mixer on low speed, add flour mixture to butter mixture in thirds, alternating with molasses mixture, beginning and ending with flour mixture. Beat until well combined. Spoon batter over pears. Place skillet on a rimmed baking sheet.

Bake until a wooden pick inserted in center comes out clean, approximately 35 minutes. (Loosely cover with foil during last 10 minutes to prevent excess browning, if necessary.) Let cool in skillet 5 minutes. Run a knife around edge to loosen; carefully invert cake onto a flat serving plate.

SKILLET APPLES

Yield: approximately 8 servings

2	cups sugar
½	cup water
8	Pink Lady apples, peeled and cut into ½-inch-thick slices
1	cup golden raisins
1	vanilla bean, split lengthwise, seeds scraped and reserved
½	teaspoon lemon zest
1	tablespoon fresh lemon juice

In a large cast-iron skillet, bring sugar and ½ cup water to a boil over medium-high heat. Cook, without stirring, until mixture turns amber in color, 10 to 15 minutes.

Add apple, raisins, vanilla bean and reserved seeds, and lemon zest and juice, stirring to combine. Cook, stirring occasionally, until apples are just tender and sauce is slightly reduced, approximately 10 minutes. Discard vanilla bean before serving.

Serving Suggestion | Spoon this harvest-fresh topping over ice cream, coffee cakes, and pancakes.

UPSIDE DOWN APPLE CRISP CAKE

Yield: 6 to 8 servings

Crumble:
- ¼ cup firmly packed light brown sugar
- ¼ cup old-fashioned oats
- 3 tablespoons unsalted butter, softened
- 2 tablespoons all-purpose flour
- ⅛ teaspoon kosher salt

Cake:
- ½ cup plus ⅓ cup unsalted butter, softened and divided
- 1 cup plus ¾ cup firmly packed light brown sugar, divided
- ¾ teaspoon ground cinnamon, divided
- ¾ teaspoon ground nutmeg, divided
- 2 large apples, peeled and thinly sliced
- 1 large egg
- 1⅓ cups all-purpose flour
- 2 teaspoons baking powder
- ½ teaspoon kosher salt
- ⅓ cup whole milk
- 1 teaspoon vanilla extract

Preheat oven to 350°.

FOR CRUMBLE:

In a small bowl, stir together brown sugar, oats, butter, flour, and salt until crumbly.

FOR CAKE:

In a 10-inch cast-iron skillet, melt ⅓ cup butter over medium heat. Add ¾ cup brown sugar, ¼ teaspoon cinnamon, and ¼ teaspoon nutmeg, stirring to combine. Cook, stirring occasionally, until thickened, approximately 8 minutes. Remove from heat. Place apple slices over caramel in skillet. Set aside.

In a large bowl, beat remaining ½ cup butter and remaining 1 cup brown sugar at medium speed with a mixer until fluffy, 3 to 4 minutes, stopping to scrape sides of bowl. Add egg, beating to combine.

In a medium bowl, stir together flour, baking powder, salt, and remaining ½ teaspoon each cinnamon and nutmeg. With mixer on low speed, add flour mixture to butter mixture in thirds, alternating with milk, beginning and ending with flour mixture. Beat in vanilla until combined. Spoon batter over apples in skillet, smoothing top with an offset spatula. Sprinkle crumble over batter.

Bake until a wooden pick inserted in center comes out clean, approximately 40 minutes. Let cool in pan 10 minutes. Carefully invert onto a flat serving plate.

APPLE CHEDDAR PIE WEDGES

Yield: 8 servings

1   (14.1-ounce) package refrigerated
    piecrusts (2 sheets), divided
2   cups peeled and thinly sliced Pink Lady
    apple (about 1½ apples)
¾   cup shredded sharp white Cheddar
    cheese, divided
2   tablespoons firmly packed light brown
    sugar
1   tablespoon all-purpose flour
1½ teaspoons fresh lemon juice
¼   teaspoon ground nutmeg
⅛   teaspoon ground ginger
Pinch kosher salt
1   tablespoon unsalted butter,
    cut into 8 equal pieces

Preheat oven to 350°. Spray a 9-inch cast-iron wedge pan with nonstick cooking spray.

On a lightly floured surface, roll 1 piecrust into a 12-inch circle. Cut piecrust into 8 equal triangles. Press 1 triangle into bottom and up sides of each well in prepared pan.

In a medium bowl, stir together apple, ½ cup cheese, brown sugar, flour, lemon juice, nutmeg, ginger, and salt. Divide apple mixture evenly among wells; top each with 1 piece of butter.

On a lightly floured surface, cut remaining piecrust into 8 equal triangles. Top wells with remaining triangles, pressing edges to seal. Crimp as desired. Using a sharp knife, pierce top of each well 3 times. Sprinkle evenly with remaining ¼ cup cheese.

Bake until crust is golden brown, approximately 30 minutes. Let cool slightly in pan. Serve warm or at room temperature.

SWEET POTATO SKILLET COBBLER

Yield: approximately 8 servings

Dough:
1¼ cups all-purpose flour
1   teaspoon kosher salt
1   teaspoon sugar
8   tablespoons cold unsalted butter, cubed
3 to 4 tablespoons whole buttermilk, chilled
1   large egg
1   teaspoon water
2   teaspoons sugar

Filling:
2   medium sweet potatoes, peeled and
        halved lengthwise
½   cup sweetened dried cranberries,
        chopped
½   cup toasted pecans, chopped
½   cup firmly packed light brown sugar
½   cup maple syrup
1   teaspoon orange zest
1   tablespoon fresh lemon juice
¾   teaspoon ground cinnamon
¼   teaspoon ground nutmeg
⅛   teaspoon salt
2   tablespoons cold unsalted butter, cubed

Preheat oven to 375°.

FOR DOUGH:

In a medium bowl, stir together flour, salt, and sugar. Using a fork or pastry blender, cut butter into flour mixture until mixture resembles coarse crumbs.

Add buttermilk, 1 tablespoon at a time, stirring until a dough forms. Turn dough out onto a lightly floured surface; shape into a disk. Cover tightly with plastic wrap and refrigerate until firm, at least 30 minutes.

FOR FILLING:

Cut sweet potato crosswise into ½-inch-thick slices. In a large saucepan, place sweet potato; add water to cover by 2 inches. Bring to a boil over high heat; cook until slightly tender, approximately 2 minutes. Drain.

In a large bowl, stir together cranberries, pecans, brown sugar, maple syrup, zest, lemon juice, cinnamon, nutmeg, and salt. Gently stir in sweet potato. Spoon mixture into a 10-inch cast-iron skillet. Sprinkle with butter.

On a lightly floured surface, roll dough into a 12-inch circle. Cut dough into 12 strips; arrange over sweet potato mixture in a lattice design. Trim ends to fit. In a small bowl, whisk together egg and 1 teaspoon water; brush over dough. Sprinkle with sugar.

Bake until golden brown and bubbly, approximately 30 minutes. Serve warm.

CORNMEAL CAKE WITH RED GRAPES

Yield: approximately 10 servings

Cake:
- 2 tablespoons unsalted butter
- 2 (8.5-ounce) packages corn muffin mix, such as Jiffy
- 2 large eggs, lightly beaten
- ⅔ cup whole buttermilk
- ¼ cup sugar
- 1 teaspoon orange zest
- 1 teaspoon vanilla extract
- 1½ cups red seedless grapes, halved
- 1 tablespoon turbinado sugar

Glaze:
- 2 tablespoons whole buttermilk
- 1 teaspoon orange zest
- 2 tablespoons fresh orange juice
- 2 cups confectioners' sugar

Preheat oven to 350°.

FOR CAKE:

In a deep 10-inch cast-iron skillet, add butter. Place in oven until butter melts, approximately 5 minutes. Remove from oven, and set aside.

In a large bowl, stir together corn muffin mix, eggs, buttermilk, sugar, zest, and vanilla until well combined. Spoon half of batter into prepared skillet. Scatter ½ cup grapes evenly over batter. Top with remaining batter, remaining 1 cup grapes, and turbinado sugar.

Bake until a wooden pick inserted in center comes out clean, 25 to 30 minutes. Let cool in skillet 5 minutes. Run a knife around edges to loosen; transfer to a wire rack.

FOR GLAZE:

In a small bowl, whisk together buttermilk, orange zest and juice, and confectioners' sugar until smooth. Drizzle glaze over cake.

CAST-IRON CARE
TIPS FOR RESPECTING AND PROTECTING YOUR FAVORITE HEIRLOOMS

– DO –

USE IT OFTEN
The more you use your beloved cast-iron skillets, the more seasoned their finishes become. Be sure to clean your pans as soon as they're cool enough to handle.

KEEP IT DRY
After washing, dry your cookware immediately to ward off rust. Heat it on the stove over low heat for approximately 5 minutes. While the pan is still warm, rub or brush on a light coating of oil. Let cool completely.

STORAGE TIP
Be conservative when applying oil to your pans for storing and seasoning. Using too much can result in a sticky residue. To remove any residue, heat your pan over medium heat. Using a folded paper towel or cloth, carefully rub in 1 tablespoon oil at a time until the surface is smooth. Store in a cool, dry place.

– DON'T –

DON'T leave a pan unattended on the stove.
DON'T use harsh abrasives.
DON'T use soap (if you can help it).
DON'T submerge your pans in water.
DON'T place your pans in the dishwasher.
DON'T put cast-iron pans away wet.

RESIDUE-REMOVAL TIP

1. Scrub the pan with a stiff-bristle brush and hot soapy water to remove any rust or buildup. Rinse well, and dry completely.

2. Use a cloth or paper towel to rub a light coating of oil on the pan, inside and out.

3. Place a sheet of aluminum foil or a rimmed baking sheet on the lower rack of your oven to catch drips. Place the oiled pan upside down on middle rack of the oven, and bake at 350° for approximately 1 hour.

4. Turn off the oven, and let your pan cool in the oven. Repeat as necessary until finish is restored. Store in a cool, dry place.

INDEX

Chocolate Cobbler, page 16, courtesy Bea Farmer

Chocolate-Pecan Snickerdoodle Skillet Cookie, page 23, Pecan Upside Down Cake, page 110, and Skillet Apple Streusel Cakes, page 56, courtesy Christy Jordan